Words
Stop *to* You *from*
Falling *to*
Hell

HS PRESS

Words *to* Stop *from* You Falling *to* Hell

EL CANTARE

Ryuho Okawa

HS PRESS

Contents

Words to Stop You from Falling to Hell

Words to Stop You from Falling to Hell

$$\textbf{1}$$

There is no good future for

those without faith.

$$\left(2\right)$$

Hell is a manifestation of what is in your mind.

$\textcircled{3}$

Those who deny spiritual beings

are slaves to money.

Who are you if you take away

your worldly status and job title?

(5)

What is recorded in the diary of

your mind will be copied into

the record book kept by Yama,

the Special Judge of Hell,

to make the judgment.

$\textcircled{6}$

In hell, there are two kinds of
ogres: One is the classic example
of a villain, and the other protects
Buddha's Truth. The former are
punished and the latter are the
Punisher sent by Buddha.

(7)

Buddha teaches that the world
of hell is also governed by
Buddha's Truth and the Law of
Cause and Effect.

(8)

It is best that good cause leads to good results, and bad cause leads to bad results within this lifetime. If not, the world of hell will expand.

9

He who gives will be given,

and he who takes will be taken;

this is the law of the Real World.

(10)

Therefore, you won't lose anything by giving love, and you won't gain anything from deceiving and taking from others.

(11)

The love between men and women can take people to either heaven or hell, depending on whether the relationship is based on giving or taking from the perspective of Buddha's Truth.

(12)

The Hell of the Bloody Pond

exists to this day. You will go there

if your self-control and true love

succumb to animal instinct.

To avoid going to the Hell of the Bloody Pond, practice the Meditation on Skeletonization. Even if the person you desire decomposes into bones, will you still love their soul?

$$\textcircled{14}$$

The Hell of the Bloody Pond is an entrance level of hell. If you can't get out of there, it means you are a vicious sexual offender.

In the Hell of the Bloody Pond

you are tested, "Is your

true nature human or animal?"

(16)

Then, if you are judged to be extremely animalistic, you will be sent to the Hell of Beasts or the world of animals.

In the Hell of Beasts, you will turn into an animal, but your face will sometimes glitch and the face you had when you were a human appears.

(18)

A lazy person will become a skinny horse and walk endlessly along a maze-like mountain path carrying heavy sacks on its back.

A highly aggressive person will become a wild beast and will continue to assault other animals until it realizes how meaningless killing is.

⑳

Herbivores and small animals that are preyed upon will continue to suffer in fear. Sometimes you will even spot a zebra imprinted with the words, "Article 9 of the Constitution" of Japan*— the stripes reflect their desire to protect themselves through camouflage.

(21)

Those who were too timid to do

useful work and sustain their

families are constantly on the

run, hopping around like rabbits.

Those who just screamed, shouted, and made a racket without contributing to society are turned into monkeys and they flock together. (They were, for example, groupies who supported shallow music.)

$$\left(23\right)$$

Those who were filthy, unable to clean, wash, and organize, are rolling around in mud like pigs.

I caught a glimpse of the spirit

of a former actress who had left

her house dirty with piles of

unwashed underwear and even

used sanitary products.

(Of course, she has become

a pig covered in dung.)

(25)

I saw a group of wild dogs running around. When alive, they were men and women, who had gone out every night committing crimes.

I saw dozens of snakes tangling up with one another as they slithered on the ground. When alive, they were people who had been taken over by love affairs, alcohol, drugs, and stimulants.

I found many foxes in hell. When alive, they were men and women who had worked in the nightlife, gambling, and sex trade industries.

Among the foxes in hell,

I saw the cunning ones

possessing evil psychics and

religious leaders in this world,

and expanding their group.

(29)

I saw vampire bats flying about the caves in hell. When alive, they were people who engaged in work that exploited others like bloodsuckers.

I saw a pack of wild boars running

straight off a cliff into the river.

When alive, they were young

motorcycle gang members.

$$\textbf{(31)}$$

I saw a toad being swallowed

whole by a giant green snake.

When alive, the toad was a man

who had lied and seduced women

one after another. One of those

women became a snake out of

resentment after death.

(32)

I saw a man, who had repeatedly borrowed money and kept going bankrupt during his lifetime, being devoured by piranhas in a pond until he was reduced to bones. These piranhas were his moneylenders.

(33)

I saw sons and daughters, who
had caused nothing but trouble to
their parents during their lifetime,
being swallowed into the sandpit
of the antlion and eaten away.

I saw herons deceiving and fighting each other over small fish. When alive, they were people who scammed others.

(35)

I saw criminals atoning for their
sins by serving as guard dogs.
When alive, they committed
theft and robbery.

I saw flocks of chickens having their heads chopped off, one by one, by the axes of Punishers. When alive, they were a bunch of soldiers who executed the civilians.

(37)

I saw a nest of mice munching
and nibbling on the pillars
of a temple, and that's when
Punishers appeared, smashing
them into bits with their iron
bats. When alive, these mice
were people who leeched off
their parents and government.

I saw small spiders gathering around the carcass of an animal. When alive, these spiders were people who pestered others for spare change. Suddenly, a fireball fell from the sky and burned them all to a crisp.

From a pond of dung and urine appeared many worms about 6 feet long. When alive, they were the LGBTQ people who had anal sex.

$$\textbf{40}$$

Black crows swooped down and were plucking the hairs off the backs of animals. Then, a Black Punisher and a White Punisher, who had transformed into giant pandas and were breathing fire, burned the bad crows to a crisp. When alive, the crows were people who harassed and threatened others to get what they wanted.

On the right side of the
Bloody Pond, I began to see
the Mountain of Needles with
a gentle slope. Thick syringe
needles, 2 to 12 inches long,
were sticking out of the ground.

In an area of every 10 feet square, at least 50 needles were sticking out from the ground. Punishers wearing tall iron *geta* (sandals) were driving the sinners to the top of the mountain as they swung their iron bats around.

Sinners are not only criminals.

All actions that go against

Buddha's Truth based on what

you sense through your eyes,

ears, nose, tongue, tactile body,

and mind (the six sense organs),

will be judged as sins.

Those who lived 20,000 days on earth and did 10 bad things a day will be pierced a total of 200,000 times by needles and covered in blood. Some may collapse and have their entire body pierced by needles before reaching the summit.
The Punishers will mercilessly pull them back up on their feet and make them walk again.

At the summit, sinners will find however little open space they can and apologize to God or Buddha for the many evil deeds they committed in their lives. The sins that are committed with the physical body will essentially return as physical pain, and this is their punishment.

46

The sinners will be chased down
to the foot of the mountain by the
Punishers, and will repeatedly climb
up and down the mountain until
the Punishers say it's enough. Most
sinners will continually shed tears
of regret as they are shocked to learn
how severely they are punished for
bad-mouthing others, using violence,
lying, and doing shameful acts. Every
disrespectful act they did to their
parents and teachers will certainly be
judged as a sin.

Beyond the Mountain of Needles, there stands a steeper mountain. This mountain is densely covered with spikes of sword blades. Sinners who did not repent enough in the Mountain of Needles will be made to climb this steeper mountain that is 3,000 to 6,000 feet high as they are slashed by swords.

As the hideous-looking sinners are bleeding all over and chased on this Sword Mountain, they begin to forget their titles, status, fame, and awards they had when they were alive. All they can hear are the Punishers yelling at them. Hundreds of Red, Blue, Green, Yellow, Black, White, and Brown Punishers are acting as prison torturers.

They will be slashed by swords
until their sword cuts reach the
number of sins they committed
knowingly and unknowingly
while they were alive.

The greater the position you had and the more people you brought suffering to, the heavier your sin will be. Liars will have their tongues yanked out by 30-inch iron pliers. Those who always chased after good-looking women will have their eyeballs gouged out. And some who practiced bad politics will be cut into two at the waist.

One time, I saw sinful people being boiled in large cauldrons; some in hot water and some in oil. Oil gets hotter than water, which means the people immersed in oil are more sinful.

In these cauldrons were officials of the Ministry of Finance and the National Tax Agency who made people suffer by imposing heavy taxes. Politicians, judges, and lawyers who oppressed right religions were in there too. Malicious lawyers who belonged to the Network of Lawyers Against Spiritual Sales in Japan were being simmered in the hottest oil.

One time, I saw the Hell of Black Ropes. People who made wrong laws, conducted wrong trials, or engaged in wrong medical activities during their lifetime were marked by inked ropes on their naked bodies and sawed by Punishers. Doctors who talked big about conducting the most advanced medical practices were sawn with electric saws by Punishers disguised as surgeons.

(53)

One time, I came across a pack of hungry ghosts. They were like a large army of zombies, assaulting and devouring a military general, who had starved his people by waging war after war when alive.

I saw people who suffered from famine when alive turned into swarms of locusts, attacked the royal family, and reduced them to bones.

One time, I saw bankers, who had refused to give out loans or forcibly retracted loans one-sidedly when alive, have their eyeballs and intestines gouged out by vultures with their beaks.

（56）

One time, I saw a man, who had made money through investment scams when alive, have his whole body devoured by the ghosts of his victims, who were like a swarm of termites.

One time, I saw people in scam groups, who had deceived elderly people when alive, being attacked by countless poisonous blowfish in a fish farm pond.

(58)

One time, I saw a man who had

spoken ill of Buddha when alive

have his hands tied to a tree

branch, be skinned alive

by black ravens, and have his

flesh eaten by wolves.

One time, I saw a man who,

when alive, called Jesus Christ

a weak God and his martyred

disciples idiots, be put on a cross,

forced to wear a crown of thorns

and hammered with a large nail.

He seemed to be a priest who had

abandoned his faith.

60

One time, I witnessed a man, who had stolen a Buddha statue and sold it off when alive, be turned into a crocodile and have its skin used to make a handbag.

(61)

One time, I saw believers of
a misguided religion sinking
into quicksand in the desert;
they were screaming, "It burns,
it burns!" in the Hell of the
Scorching Heat.

One time, I saw believers of a misguided religion be turned into small worms and tossed into a pond. A large number of worms were swarmed by vicious fish and devoured.

One time, a miser had been turned into a monkey. There was a hollowed-out coconut with rice inside, tethered to a rope. The monkey stuck its hand in the small hole to grab the rice and refused to let it go. Then, a hunter came along and the monkey, unable to escape, was shot dead.

One time, a praying mantis was being watched by a frog which was being watched by a snake. When the mantis was eaten by the frog, the frog was then swallowed by the snake. At that moment, an eagle snatched the snake with its talons and flew far up into the sky.

A person who was a habitual shoplifter had died. In the afterlife, he was put on an operating table and had many of his organs removed as an organ donor.

One time, a miser dropped gold coins into the river. He dove down to gather the coins and held them close to his chest, but he could not come up because of the heavy weight of the coins.

One time, I saw Christian and Muslim armies fighting each other in the desert. It was the Crusades. Both armies fell into the hot desert hole. Then, a 100-foot-wide pterosaur appeared in the sky and blew fire onto them, burning them to a crisp.

(68)

One time, the army of the Mongol Empire (Yuan dynasty) invaded Europe. Then, the Black Plague came and killed two-thirds of the European population. In hell, a large army of rats and a large army of cockroaches appeared. They were the souls of the dead. Hundreds of white elephants appeared and crushed the rats and cockroaches as they stampeded their way through.

(69)

I saw Europe freeze in the near future as it was hit by a cold wave. The hell of Europe also became covered in snow. At the entrance of their frozen town hung a sign that read, "Greta's Town."

There was a town in hell with a sign that read "Heroes' Town." It was inhabited by the crews of the B-29s that raided Tokyo and the forces that dropped atomic bombs on Hiroshima and Nagasaki. I saw newly developed nuclear bombs being dropped on the town and the inhabitants experiencing the Hell of Great Scorching Heat and the Hell of Agonizing Cries. I think this was also part of a vision of the near future.

Hitler and Stalin dueled in hell, pistol to pistol. After firing their guns, both men fell further down to the bottom of the well. Nearby, a well had already been dug for Saddam Hussein.

The Japanese gods didn't take responsibility for Japan's defeat in World War II. *Takamagahara* [the spiritual realm of Japanese Shinto gods] became a den of *yokai* [monsters and goblins], and the Japanese people and soldiers, who died in the war and fell to hell, were running about in the flames and suffering from starvation for decades.

A Ukrainian fox and a Russian bear are in a fight. The ancestors of those countries who had already fallen to hell are waiting for them to fall. They are getting ready to cook them into fox and bear dishes.

At the bottom of the hell of North Korea, a venomous spider known as the "Great General" has made a large nest in a cave. Its webs also stretch out and entangle the North Korean leaders in this world.

Deep underground in China, the grim reaper had built a virus research facility. The grim reaper was boasting aloud that he would rule the whole world.

Deep underground in the United States of America, the white men who massacred the indigenous people are gathering and researching several ways to wage Armageddon [the final war].

(77)

To prevent yourself from falling
to hell, you need to have the
right faith in God or Buddha.
If you believe in materialism,
atheism, the philosophy of no
soul, or scientism, you cannot
return to the heavenly world.

The light of the Spiritual Sun does not reach hell because of the dark clouds formed by the inhabitants' thoughts. Hell extends from the shallow part, where the sky is a faded gray color, to the deepest part, where it is pitch-black as if coal tar was poured in. Hell is divided into many layers based on the weight of people's sins.

(79)

Those who had slandered Buddha or persecuted the right teachings will have their basic Buddha-nature frozen. In other words, they are not permitted to enter heaven or paradise.

(80)

Those who did not repent of their

sins even in the torments of hell

will fall deeper, one level at a time.

The most wicked and sinister will not even be given the chance to be judged by the court of Yama. They will fall headfirst into the Abysmal Hell.

(82)

In the Abysmal Hell, you cannot
see others or hear their voices.
Like dangerous criminals, they
are isolated in the depths of
a well. When alive, they were
ruthless politicians, thinkers
who spread wrong ideas, or
leaders of Satanism.

(83)

What's worse, those who have been

in the pit of hell for thousands

or tens of thousands of years and

did not even self-reflect become

devils. They are plotting a rebellion

against God and some are even

gathering demons as their minions.

84

Devils and demons are trying to expand hell on earth by controlling the minds of living people who are powerful and influential. They can do so when the wavelength of those people's minds attunes to theirs.

To protect yourself from devils

controlling your mind and body,

it is important to reflect on

yourself, have gratitude, and pray

to God or Buddha every day.

86

Greed, anger, foolishness, conceit, doubt, and wrong views are the devil's tools to control humans.

That is why it is important

to desire little and know

contentment. A peaceful mind is

necessary. You should believe that

your guardian and guiding spirits

are always watching over you from

the heavenly world.

(88)

A conceited mind is the mind of
tengu. Once you are conceited as a
seeker of enlightenment, you are
on the way to downfall. Having
knowledge and information is not
the same as being enlightened.
Therefore, journalism based
on skepticism will never create
Buddha Land Utopia.

A high educational background, high income, and admirable looks do not prove you are a god. What proves that you are a person close to God and a disciple of Buddha are humility, continued effort, a kind attitude toward others, and real love.

90

Speak right words, take right action, live righteously, do right work, and think each day about how to bring light to the world.

Those who killed the Savior or Buddha shall never be forgiven. Neither will national law, political beliefs, or the mass media's opinions save them as they are meaningless in the other world.

Attacking the family or the close

associates of the Savior or Buddha

is a common tactic of devils.

Those who obstruct the spreading

of Buddha's Truth, whether they

be living people or spirits, will be

charged with heavier sins.

(93)

Those who schemed to dissolve a
right religion or brought chaos to
it using worldly power, the power
of the mass media, and such,
will fall into the Hell of Great
Agonizing Cries or the Abysmal
Hell. The same goes for those
who spread evil religions.

Those who sacrificed their lives

for the love of the Lord God, to

serve the Lord God, and to protect

the Lord God cannot be burned

with the raging inferno of hell,

slashed with the swords of hell, or

destroyed by any catastrophes.

95

Anyone who used the Lord out of their desire to protect themselves, to attain worldly self-realization, or to be respected in this world, and also tried to evade their own responsibility cannot escape the eternal flames of hell, even if they claim they are gods, buddhas, angels, or bodhisattvas.

Those who sacrificed themselves

for the sake of El Cantare and

seemingly lived a miserable life

in a worldly sense will surely have

angels or bodhisattvas come to

save them in the afterlife.

Having 99% faith is not enough.

Buddha's Truth and the spiritual

Truth are everything.

Aim to have 100% faith.

Even if you are met with a

natural disaster or great war,

protect your faith in the Lord.

This world is a temporary world.

Protecting yourself who believes

in God will ultimately

protect everything.

Spreading the Laws of
El Cantare will eliminate hell
and build Buddha Land Utopia
in this world.

Always have faith in the Lord through your past, present, and future lives. Even when the space age comes, believe that the Laws of El Cantare rule the entire universe.

TRANSLATOR'S NOTE

*Some Japanese people believe that Japan can maintain peace as long as it adheres to Article 9 of the Japanese Constitution, which prohibits the country from having a military.

Afterword and Commentary

By reading *The Laws of Hell*, *The Hell Monk*, and now this book, *Words to Stop You from Falling to Hell*, you have probably gotten a general idea of hell.

The content of this book has enough details to write a story about a journey through the world of hell, so I wrote each phrase in as much detail. I hope you will use many of my other publications as references to help you understand this book.

Reading this book aloud to anyone who might be falling to hell or who has already fallen would have the same effect as reciting the sutras.

Lastly, I would like to add that, the Lord, Buddha, Savior, Lord God, and El Cantare mentioned in this book are all essentially the same Being.

> *Ryuho Okawa*
> *Master and CEO of Happy Science Group*
> *January 24, 2023*

ABOUT THE AUTHOR

Founder and CEO of Happy Science Group.

Ryuho Okawa was born on July 7th, 1956, in Tokushima, Japan. After graduating from the University of Tokyo with a law degree, he joined a Tokyo-based trading house. While working at its New York headquarters, he studied international finance at the Graduate Center of the City University of New York. In 1981, he attained Great Enlightenment and became aware that he is El Cantare with a mission to bring salvation to all humankind.

In 1986, he established Happy Science. It now has members in 178 countries across the world, with more than 700 branches and temples as well as 10,000 missionary houses around the world.

He has given over 3,500 lectures (of which more than 150 are in English) and published over 3,200 books (of which more than 600 are Spiritual Interview Series), and many are translated into 42 languages. Along with *The Laws of the Sun* and *The Laws of Hell*, many of the books have become best sellers or million sellers. To date, Happy Science has produced 28 movies under his supervision. He has given the original story and concept and is also the Executive Producer. He has also composed music and written lyrics for over 450 pieces.

Moreover, he is the Founder of Happy Science University and Happy Science Academy (Junior and Senior High School), Founder and President of the Happiness Realization Party, Founder and Honorary Headmaster of Happy Science Institute of Government and Management, Founder of IRH Press Co., Ltd., and the Chairperson of NEW STAR PRODUCTION Co., Ltd. and ARI Production Co., Ltd.

BOOKS BY RYUHO OKAWA

The Latest Titles

One More Step Forward

The Invincible Thinking to get you through tough times

Paperback • 256 pages • $17.95
ISBN: 978-1-958655-25-2 (May 7, 2025)

Success in life is determined not by our circumstances but by our mindset and how we think. In this book, the author reveals from his first-hand experience how the spirit of self-help can create new values.

Ryuho Okawa is a true self-made man with an indomitable spirit to bring happiness to all humankind. His drive to keep moving forward by taking steady steps through the power of discipline has led to the publication of over 3,200 books in just 37 years. Unlock the keys to lifelong growth and success by reading this book.

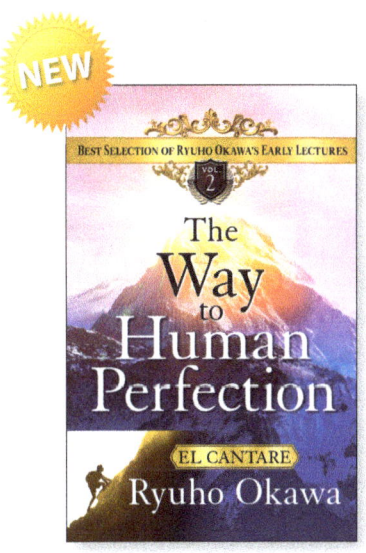

The Way to Human Perfection

Best Selection of Ryuho Okawa's Early Lectures (Volume 2)

Paperback • 200 pages • $17.95
ISBN: 978-1-958655-20-7 (Oct. 22, 2024)

The path to enlightenment starts from understanding 'the eternal viewpoint of life.' Through each chapter, Ryuho Okawa navigates us to shift the perspective of ourselves from a 'finite self' living a limited life to an 'eternal self' living an eternal life.

If we can recognize that our soul is eternal and that every thought and action has consequences, then we can realize that caring and bringing joy to others are the keys to true happiness and success.

Walking the path towards higher enlightenment is the source of improving character so we can build better relationships with others. It is the new value to unlock a bright future.

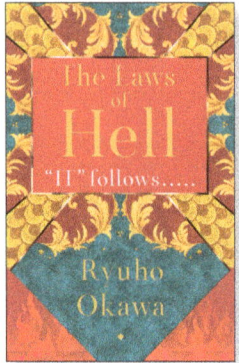

The Laws of Hell

"IT" follows.....

Paperback • 264 pages • $17.95
ISBN: 978-1-958655-04-7 (May 1, 2023)

Whether you believe it or not, the Spirit World and hell do exist, and unfortunately, 1 in 2 people are falling to hell. To stop hell from spreading and to save the souls of all human beings, Ryuho Okawa has compiled vital teachings in this book. This publication marks his 3,100th book and is the one and only comprehensive Truth about the modern hell.

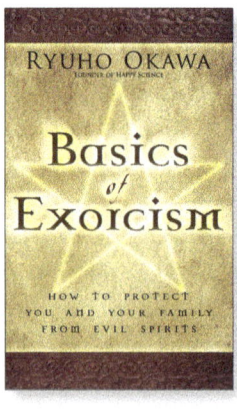

Basics of Exorcism

How to Protect You and Your Family from Evil Spirits

Paperback • 130 pages • $14.95
ISBN: 979-8887370408 (Feb. 27, 2015)

Learn about how to protect yourself and your family from the influences of evil spirits and demons. Discover the spiritual reasons for issues such as personality disorder and schizophrenia from a spiritual leader with extraordinary psychic abilities.

The Truth about the Spirit World

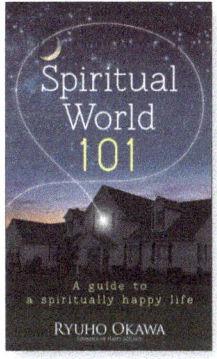

Spiritual World 101
A Guide to a Spiritually Happy Life
Paperback • 184 pages • $14.95
ISBN: 978-1-941779-43-9 (Mar. 25, 2015)

This book is a spiritual guidebook that will answer all your questions about the spiritual world, with illustrations and diagrams explaining your guardian spirit and the secrets of God and Buddha. By reading this book, you will be able to understand the true meaning of life and find happiness in everyday life.

My Journey through the Spirit World
A True Account of My Experiences of the Hereafter
Paperback • 224 pages • $15.95
ISBN: 978-1-942125-41-9 (Jul. 25, 2018)

In this book, Ryuho Okawa shares surprising facts about the afterworld. This unique and authentic guide to the spirit world will awaken us to the truth of life and death, and show us how we should start living so that we can return to a bright world of heaven.

The Truth about Spiritual Phenomena
Life's Q&A with El Cantare
Paperback • 180 pages • $17.95
ISBN: 978-1-958655-0-92 (Oct. 27, 2023)

These are the records of Ryuho Okawa's answers to 26 questions related to spiritual phenomena and mental health, which were conducted live during his early public lectures with the audience. With his great spiritual ability, he revealed the unknown spiritual Truth behind the spiritual phenomena.

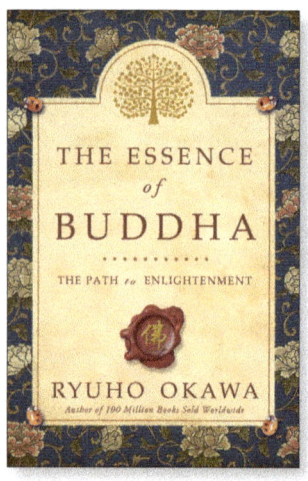

The Essence of Buddha

The Path to Enlightenment

Paperback • 208 pages • $14.95
ISBN: 978-1-942125-06-8 (Oct. 1, 2016)

In this book, Ryuho Okawa imparts in simple and accessible language his wisdom about the essence of Shakyamuni Buddha's philosophy of life and enlightenment—teachings that have been inspiring people all over the world for over 2,500 years. By offering a new perspective on core Buddhist thoughts that have long been cloaked in mystique, Okawa brings these teachings to life for modern people. *The Essence of Buddha* distills a way of life that anyone can practice to achieve a life of self-growth, compassionate living, and true happiness.

The True Eightfold Path

Guideposts for Self-Innovation

Paperback • 272 pages • $16.95
ISBN: 978-1-942125-80-8 (Mar. 30, 2021)

This book explains how we can apply the Eightfold Path, one of the main pillars of Shakyamuni Buddha's teachings, as everyday guideposts in the modern age to achieve self-innovation to live better and make positive changes in these uncertain times.

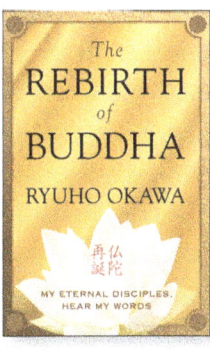

The Rebirth of Buddha

My Eternal Disciples, Hear My Words

Paperback • 280 pages • $17.95
ISBN: 978-1-942125-95-2 (Aug. 15, 2022)

These are the messages of Buddha who has returned to this modern age as promised to His eternal beloved disciples. They are in simple words and poetic style, yet contain profound messages. Once you start reading these passages, your soul will be replenished as the plant absorbs the water, and you will remember why you chose this era to be born into with Buddha. Listen to the voices of your Eternal Master and awaken to your calling.

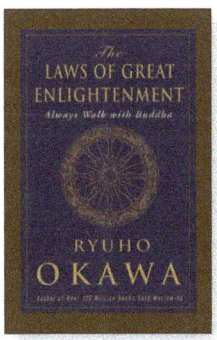

The Laws of Great Enlightenment

Always Walk with Buddha

Paperback • 232 pages • $17.95
ISBN: 978-1-942125-62-4 (Nov. 7, 2019)

In this book, Ryuho Okawa explains essential Buddhist tenets and how to put them into practice. Enlightenment is not just an abstract idea but one that everyone can experience to some extent. Okawa offers a solid basis of reason and an intellectual understanding of Buddhist concepts.

The first three volumes of the Laws Series, *The Laws of the Sun*, *The Golden Laws*, and *The Laws of Eternity* make a trilogy that completes the basic framework of the teachings of God's Truths. *The Laws of the Sun* discusses the structure of God's Laws, *The Golden Laws* expounds on the doctrine of time, and *The Laws of Eternity* reveals the nature of space.

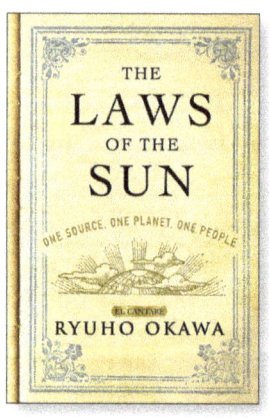

The Laws of the Sun

One Source, One Planet, One People

Paperback • 288 pages • $15.95
ISBN: 978-1-942125-43-3 (Oct. 25, 2018)

IMAGINE IF YOU COULD ASK GOD why He created this world and about the spiritual laws He used to shape us and everything around us. If we could understand His designs and intentions, we could discover what our goals in life should be and whether our actions move us closer to those goals or farther away.

At a young age, a spiritual calling prompted Ryuho Okawa to outline what he innately understood to be universal truths for all humankind. In *The Laws of the Sun*, Okawa outlines these laws of the universe and provides a road map for living one's life with greater purpose and meaning. In this powerful book, Ryuho Okawa reveals the transcendent nature of consciousness and the secrets of the multidimensional universe as well as the meaning of humans that exist within it. By understanding the different stages of love and following the Buddhist Eightfold Path, he believes we can speed up our eternal process of development. *The Laws of the Sun* shows the way to realize true happiness—a happiness that continues from this world through the other.

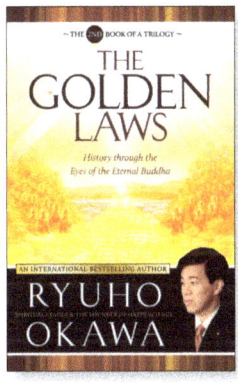

The Golden Laws

History through the Eyes of
the Eternal Buddha

E-book • 204 pages • $13.99
ISBN: 978-1-941779-82-8 (Sep. 24, 2015)

Throughout history, Great Guiding Spirits have been present on Earth in both the East and the West at crucial points in human history to further our spiritual development. *The Golden Laws* reveals how the Divine Plan has been unfolding on Earth, and outlines 5,000 years of the secret history of humankind. Once we understand the true course of history, through past, present, and into the future, we cannot help but become aware of the significance of our spiritual mission in the present age.

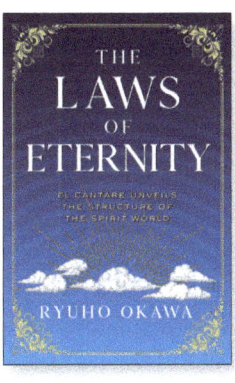

The Laws of Eternity

El Cantare Unveils the Structure of
the Spirit World

Paperback • 224 pages • $17.95
ISBN: 978-1-958655-16-0 (May 15, 2024)

"Where do we come from and where do we go after death?" This unparalleled book offers us complete answers to life's most important questions that we all are confronted with at some point or another. This book reveals the eternal mysteries and the ultimate secrets of Earth's Spirit Group that have been covered by the veil of legends and myths. Encountering the long-hidden Eternal Truths that are revealed for the first time in human history will change the way you live your life now.

WHO IS EL CANTARE?

El Cantare means "the Light of the Earth." He is the Supreme God of the Earth who has been guiding humankind since the beginning of Genesis, and He is the Creator of the universe. He is whom Jesus called Father and Muhammad called Allah, and is *Ame-no-Mioya-Gami*, Japanese Father God. Different parts of El Cantare's core consciousness have descended to Earth in the past, once as Alpha and another as Elohim. His branch spirits, such as Shakyamuni Buddha and Hermes, have descended to Earth many times and helped to flourish many civilizations. To unite various religions and to integrate various fields of study in order to build a new civilization on Earth, a part of the core consciousness has descended to Earth as Master Ryuho Okawa.

Alpha is a part of the core consciousness of El Cantare who descended to Earth around 330 million years ago. Alpha preached Earth's Truths to harmonize and unify Earth-born humans and space people who came from other planets.

Elohim is a part of the core consciousness of El Cantare who descended to Earth around 150 million years ago. He gave wisdom, mainly on the differences between light and darkness, good and evil.

Ame-no-Mioya-Gami (Japanese Father God) is the Creator God and the Father God who appears in ancient literature, *Hotsuma Tsutae*. It is believed that He descended on the foothills of Mt. Fuji about 30,000 years ago and built the Fuji dynasty, which is the root of the Japanese civilization. With justice as the central pillar, Ame-no-Mioya-Gami's teachings spread to ancient civilizations of other countries in the world.

Shakyamuni Buddha was born as a prince into the Shakya clan around 2,600 years ago. When he was 29 years old, he renounced the world and sought enlightenment. He later attained Great Enlightenment and founded Buddhism.

Hermes is one of the 12 Olympian gods in Greek mythology, but the spiritual Truth is that he taught the teachings of love and progress around 4,300 years ago which became the origin of the current Western civilization. He is a hero who truly existed.

Ophealis was born in Greece around 6,500 years ago and was the leader who took an expedition as far as Egypt. He is the God of miracles, prosperity, and arts, and is known as Osiris in Egyptian mythology.

Rient Arl Croud was born as a king of the ancient Incan Empire around 7,000 years ago and taught about the mysteries of the mind. In the heavenly world, he is responsible for the interactions that take place between various planets.

Thoth was an almighty leader who built the golden age of the Atlantic civilization around 12,000 years ago. In Egyptian mythology, he is known as God Thoth.

Ra Mu was a leader who built the golden age of the civilization of Mu around 17,000 years ago. As a religious leader and a politician, he ruled by uniting religion and politics.

ABOUT HAPPY SCIENCE

Happy Science is a religious group founded on the faith in El Cantare who is the God of the Earth, and the Creator of the universe. The essence of human beings is the soul that was created by God, and we all are children of God. God is our true parent, so in our souls, we have a fundamental desire to "believe in God, love God, and get closer to God." And, we can get closer to God by living with God's Will as our own. In Happy Science, we call this the "Exploration of Right Mind." More specifically, it means to practice the Fourfold Path, which consists of "Love, Wisdom, Self-Reflection, and Progress."

Love: Love means "love that gives," or mercy. God hopes for the happiness of all people. Therefore, living with God's Will as our own means to start by practicing "love that gives."

Wisdom: God's love is boundless. It is important to learn various Truths in order to understand the heart of God.

Self-Reflection: Once you learn the heart of God and the difference between His mind and yours, you should strive to bring your own mind closer to the mind of God—that process is called self-reflection. Self-reflection also includes meditation and prayer.

Progress: Since God hopes for the happiness of all people, you should also make progress in your love, and make an effort to realize utopia in which everyone in your society, country, and eventually all humankind can become happy.

As we practice this Fourfold Path, our souls will advance toward God step by step. That is when we can attain real happiness—our souls' desire to get closer to God comes true.

In Happy Science, we conduct activities to make ourselves happy through belief in Lord El Cantare, and to spread this faith to the world and bring happiness to all. We welcome you to join our activities!

We hold events and activities to help you practice the Fourfold Path at our branches, temples, missionary centers and missionary houses

Love: We hold various volunteering activities. Our members conduct missionary work together as the greatest practice of love.

Wisdom: We offer our comprehensive collection of books of Truth, many of which are available online and at Happy Science locations. In addition, we offer numerous opportunities such as seminars or book clubs to learn the Truth.

Self-Reflection: We offer opportunities to polish your mind through self-reflection, meditation, and prayer. Many members have experienced improvement in their human relationships by changing their own minds.

Progress: We also offer seminars to enhance your power of influence. Because it is also important to do well at work to make society better, we hold seminars to improve your work and management skills.

"The True Words Spoken By Buddha"

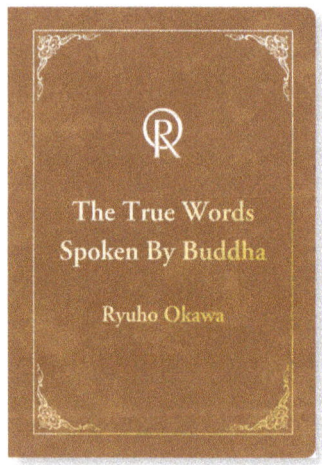

"The True Words Spoken By Buddha" is an English sutra given directly from the spirit of Shakyamuni Buddha, who is a part of Master Ryuho Okawa's subconscious. The words in this sutra are not of a mere human being but are the words of God or Buddha sent directly from the ninth dimension, which is the highest realm of the Earth's Spirit World.

"The True Words Spoken By Buddha" is an essential sutra for us to connect and live with God or Buddha's Will as our own.

MEMBERSHIPS

MEMBERSHIP

If you would like to know more about Happy Science, please consider becoming a member. Those who pledge to believe in Lord El Cantare and wish to learn more can join us.

When you become a member, you will receive the following sutras: "The True Words Spoken By Buddha," "Prayer to the Lord" and "Prayer to Guardian and Guiding Spirits."

DEVOTEE MEMBER

If you would like to learn the teachings of Happy Science and walk the path of faith, become a Devotee member who pledges devotion to the Three Treasures, which are Buddha, Dharma, and Sangha. Buddha refers to Lord El Cantare, Master Ryuho Okawa. Dharma refers to Master Ryuho Okawa's teachings. Sangha refers to Happy Science. Devoting to the Three Treasures will let your Buddha nature shine, and you will enter the path to attain true freedom of the mind.

Becoming a devotee means you become Buddha's disciple. You will discipline your mind and act to bring happiness to society.

📧 **EMAIL** OR📞 **PHONE CALL**

Please turn to the contact information page.

🔗 **ONLINE** member.happy-science.org/signup/ 🔍

CONTACT INFORMATION

Happy Science is a worldwide organization with branches and temples around the globe. For a comprehensive list, visit the worldwide directory at happy-science.org. The following are some of our main Happy Science locations:

UNITED STATES AND CANADA

New York
79 Franklin St., New York, NY 10013, USA
Phone: 1-212-343-7972
Fax: 1-212-343-7973
Email: ny@happy-science.org
Website: happyscience-usa.org

New Jersey
66 Hudson St., #2R, Hoboken, NJ 07030, USA
Phone: 1-201-313-0127
Email: nj@happy-science.org
Website: happyscience-usa.org

Chicago
33 West Higgins Rd. 4040,
South Barrington, IL 60010, USA
Phone: 1-630-937-3077
Email: chicago@happy-science.org
Website: happyscience-usa.org

Florida
5208 8th St., Zephyrhills, FL 33542, USA
Phone: 1-813-715-0000
Fax: 1-813-715-0010
Email: florida@happy-science.org
Website: happyscience-usa.org

Atlanta
1874 Piedmont Ave., NE Suite 360-C
Atlanta, GA 30324, USA
Phone: 1-404-892-7770
Email: atlanta@happy-science.org
Website: happyscience-usa.org

San Francisco
525 Clinton St.
Redwood City, CA 94062, USA
Phone & Fax: 1-650-363-2777
Email: sf@happy-science.org
Website: happyscience-usa.org

Los Angeles
1590 E. Del Mar Blvd., Pasadena,
CA 91106, USA
Phone: 1-626-395-7775
Fax: 1-626-395-7776
Email: la@happy-science.org
Website: happyscience-usa.org

Orange County
16541 Gothard St. Suite 104
Huntington Beach, CA 92647
Phone: 1-714-659-1501
Email: oc@happy-science.org
Website: happyscience-usa.org

San Diego
7841 Balboa Ave. Suite #202
San Diego, CA 92111, USA
Phone: 1-626-395-7775
Fax: 1-626-395-7776
E-mail: sandiego@happy-science.org
Website: happyscience-usa.org

Hawaii
Phone: 1-808-591-9772
Fax: 1-808-591-9776
Email: hi@happy-science.org
Website: happyscience-usa.org

Kauai
3343 Kanakolu Street, Suite 5
Lihue, HI 96766, USA
Phone: 1-808-822-7007
Fax: 1-808-822-6007
Email: kauai-hi@happy-science.org
Website: happyscience-usa.org

Toronto

845 The Queensway
Etobicoke, ON M8Z 1N6, Canada
Phone: 1-416-901-3747
Email: toronto@happy-science.org
Website: happy science.ca

Vancouver

#201-2607 East 49th Avenue,
Vancouver, BC, V5S 1J9, Canada
Phone: 1-604-437-7735
Fax: 1-604-437-7764
Email: vancouver@happy-science.org
Website: happy-science.ca

INTERNATIONAL

Tokyo

1-6-7 Togoshi, Shinagawa,
Tokyo, 142-0041, Japan
Phone: 81-3-6384-5770
Fax: 81-3-6384-5776
Email: tokyo@happy-science.org
Website: happy-science.org

London

3 Margaret St.
London, W1W 8RE United Kingdom
Phone: 44-20-7323-9255
Fax: 44-20-7323-9344
Email: eu@happy-science.org
Website: www.happyscience-uk.org

Sydney

516 Pacific Highway, Lane Cove North,
2066 NSW, Australia
Phone: 61-2-9411-2877
Fax: 61-2-9411-2822
Email: sydney@happy-science.org

Sao Paulo

Rua. Domingos de Morais 1154,
Vila Mariana, Sao Paulo SP
CEP 04010-100, Brazil
Phone: 55-11-5088-3800
Email: sp@happy-science.org
Website: happyscience.com.br

Jundiai

Rua Congo, 447, Jd. Bonfiglioli
Jundiai-CEP, 13207-340, Brazil
Phone: 55-11-4587-5952
Email: jundiai@happy-science.org

Seoul

74, Sadang-ro 27-gil,
Dongjak-gu, Seoul, Korea
Phone: 82-2-3478-8777
Fax: 82-2-3478-9777
Email: korea@happy-science.org

Taipei

No. 89, Lane 155, Dunhua N. Road,
Songshan District, Taipei City 105, Taiwan
Phone: 886-2-2719-9377
Fax: 886-2-2719-5570
Email: taiwan@happy-science.org

Taichung

No. 146, Minzu Rd., Central Dist.,
Taichung City 400001, Taiwan
Phone: 886-4-2223-3777
Email: taichung@happy-science.org

Kuala Lumpur

No 22A, Block 2, Jalil Link Jalan Jalil Jaya
2, Bukit Jalil 57000,
Kuala Lumpur, Malaysia
Phone: 60-3-8998-7877
Fax: 60-3-8998-7977
Email: malaysia@happy-science.org
Website: happyscience.org.my

Kathmandu

Kathmandu Metropolitan City,
Ward No. 15, Ring Road, Kimdol,
Sitapaila Kathmandu, Nepal
Phone: 977-1-537-2931
Email: nepal@happy-science.org

Kampala

Plot 877 Rubaga Road, Kampala
P.O. Box 34130 Kampala, Uganda
Email: uganda@happy-science.org

ABOUT HS PRESS

HS Press is an imprint of IRH Press Co., Ltd. IRH Press Co., Ltd., based in Tokyo, was founded in 1987 as a publishing division of Happy Science. IRH Press publishes religious and spiritual books, journals, and magazines and also operates broadcast and film production enterprises. For more information, visit okawabooks.com.

Follow us on:

f Facebook: Okawa Books   **⊙** Instagram: OkawaBooks

▶ Youtube: Okawa Books   **𝕐** Twitter: Okawa Books

𝓟 Pinterest: Okawa Books   **g** Goodreads: Ryuho Okawa

——— **NEWSLETTER** ———

To receive book-related news, promotions and events, please subscribe to our newsletter below.

🔗 irhpress.com/pages/subscribe

——— **AUDIO / VISUAL MEDIA** ———

YOUTUBE

PODCAST

Visit the above to learn more about Ryuho Okawa's books. Topics ranging from self-help, current affairs, spirituality, religion, and the universe.